The Surname Elphick

Susan Morris &
Wendy Bosberry-Scott

ISBN: 1540480720
ISBN-13: 978-1540480729

The question of surnames, their origins, distribution and history, lies at the heart of genealogy as well as being fascinating in its own right.

In the 1980s and 1990s, long before many genealogical sources were even indexed, let alone online, our Surname Report service provided expert assessments of the origins, history and distribution of selected British surnames, using the sources available at the time.

Now, with so many more sources available, we believe that these reports retain their value as studies of individual surnames, and so we are gradually making the Debrett Surname Archive available online and in print for the first time. Some modern indexes have been consulted to refresh and update the reports.

Debrett Ancestry Research Ltd, PO Box 379,
Winchester SO23 9YQ
Tel: 01962 841904
Email: info@debrettancestry.co.uk
Website: www.debrettancestry.co.uk

CONTENTS

Overview

The use of surnames in England began in the Norman period, when surnames were not necessarily hereditary but usually a form of description. Some described the individual's trade or profession; others were nicknames; some gave the father's Christian name; others gave the individual's place of residence or origin.

Different surnames might be used in different documents, or more than one surname given in one document. Early descriptions were fairly elaborate and by the thirteenth and fourteenth centuries these were simpler, but still variable, and indeed the instability of surnames continued until well into the seventeenth century.

Although some Normans would already have had hereditary surnames on their arrival in Britain, the passing on of a surname from generation to generation only became customary in Britain gradually during the course of the thirteenth and fourteenth centuries. At the end of this period most of the population apparently had surnames.

Variations in the spelling of a family's surname continue to be found until the present century. Before this, as most people could not read or write, the parish clerk or other official would write down the name as they heard it.

There are four main groups of surnames:

> A - Local names, which describe a person by his place of residence or origin.
> B - Occupational names, which describe a person by his trade or profession.
> C - Surnames of relationship, which refer to the given name of the father or other important relative.
> D - Nicknames or sobriquets, coined to describe a person in terms of his appearance or character.

Many surnames have uncertain origins, but the name Elphick clearly falls into Category C.

Origins and Early Examples

The name Elphick derives from the Old English personal name *Ælfhēah,* meaning 'elf high'. The surname has been found in a variety of forms during the course of our research: Alphege, Alphegh, Elfeck, Elfick, Elphic, Elphiche, Elphicke and Elvidge.

As a surname, Elphick is included in *A Dictionary of English Surnames* by the late P H Reaney, revised by R M Wilson (1995), where it is grouped with Alphege, Elfick and Elvidge. Reaney cites numerous examples of the personal name:

Ælfec	1066	Domesday Book, Hampshire
Ælfech	1066	Domesday Book, Sussex
Ælfhag	1066	Domesday Book, Nottinghamshire
Alfeg	1066	Domesday Book, Cornwall
Alfah	1066	Domesday Book, Norfolk
Elfeg	1066	Domesday Book, Derbyshire
Elfac	1066	Domesday Book, Shropshire
Alfegus	1137	E Ekwall, *Early London Personal Names* (Lund, 1947)
Elfegus de Erningeton	1166	Pipe Rolls Gloucestershire
Elphegus	c1216	*Cartulary of the Priory of St Gregory, Canterbury* (Camden Society, 3rd Series, 88, 1956) Kent
Alfeg ater Legh	1296	Subsidy Rolls, Sussex

Reaney derives all these from the Old English *Ælfhēah* ('elf high'), Alphege being a Normanised form of the name. He cites the following early examples in which the given name has become a surname:

John Elpheg	1297	Placita coram domino Rege .... 1297 (British Record Society, 19, 1898) Kent
William Alfegh	1318	A Descriptive Catalogue of Ancient Deeds (vol vi), Kent
Robert Elfegh	1526	Testimenta Cantiana (Kent Archaeological Society, 1907-8)
William Elphike	1549	Index of Wills Proved in the Rochester Consistory Court (Kent Record Society, 9, 1924)
Margaret Elvishe	1609	Yorkshire Wills

Reaney also discusses the comparable group of surnames 'Allvey, Alvey, Alvy, Elvey, Elvy and Elphee' which he derives from the Old English *Ælfwīg* ('elf war'), another given name that gave rise to a surname group:

Godric Filius Ælfuuii	c1095	D C Douglas Feudal Documents from the Abbey of Bury St Edmunds (London, 1932) Suffolk
Alfwy	1212	Liber Feodorum 3 Volumes (London, 1920-1931) Berkshire

Swein, William Alvi	1212	Curia Regis Oxfordshire
Thomas *Alfy*	1279	Rotuli Hundredorum Cambridgeshire
Simon *Elphey*	1279	Rotuli Hundredorum Devon
Adam *Alfwy*	1296	Subsidy Rolls, Sussex
Joh, Agnes *Aluy*	1327	Subsidy Rolls, Sussex
Edward *Eluy*	1327	Subsidy Rolls, Sussex

Old English *Ælfwīg* – elf war – see also Alaway, Elvey

Similarly, Reaney derives the surname Elv(e)y from the Old English *Ælfgifu* ('Elf gift'), which was again found also as a given name:

Elvey, Elvy

Elviva	1325	*A Short Calendar of Deeds relating to Norwich 1285-1306; A Calendar of Norwich Deeds 1307-1341* (Norfolk and Norwich Archaeological Society, 1903, 1915)
Richard *Elvy*	1338	Feet of Fines Yorkshire
John *Elphy*	1450	*Archaelogica Cantiana* v
Thomas *Elveve*	1488	*Index of Wills and Administrations ... in the Probate Registry at Canterbury 1396-1558 and 1640-1650* (Index Library, 50, 1920)

John *Elvew*   1518 *Index of Wills and*
                           Administrations ... in the
                           Probate Registry at Canterbury
                           1396-1558 and 1640-1650
                           (Index Library, 50, 1920)

Ernest Weekley in *The Romance of Surnames* (1914) had also noted:

> ... Elphick (*Ælfheah*) which in Norman French gave Alphege ...

In a later work (*Surnames*, published in 1927) Weekley used the surname Elphick as an example of the mutation of Old English names into Norman ones:

> Even when Anglo-Saxon names survived ... they were often affected in sound by the Norman pronunciation, for it must be remembered that, during the period of formation of our surnames, French was the official language and a considerable proportion of the population was bilingual. For instance, Alphege is the Norman form of Elphick ...

Reaney also used Elphick as an example of the same phenomenon in *The Origins of the English Surnames* (1967):

> Some Old English names have been influenced by Anglo-Norman pronunciation *eg* ...Old English *Ælfhēah* 'elf-high' has become Elfick, Elphick, Elvidge and Elvish and, from a common Norman form, Alphege.

As we have seen, Reaney discovered that the Old English personal name *Ælfhēah* continued to be in widespread use after the Norman Conquest. He found it in records for counties as far apart as Gloucestershire and Essex but early examples of the surname appear to be concentrated in Kent. Reaney concluded that the popularity of the name in this county was due largely to the veneration of St Alphege, who was Archbishop of Canterbury from 984 to 1012.

Patrick Hanks and Flavia Hodges' *Dictionary of Surnames* (Oxford, 1992), which includes names of European derivation, follows Reaney:

> **Elphick** English: from the Middle English given name *Elfegh, Alfeg,* [and] Old English *Ælfhēah,* composed of the elements *ælf* [meaning] elf and *hēah* [meaning] high. The name was sometimes bestowed in honour of St Alphege (954-1012) archbishop of Canterbury, who was stoned to death by the Danes, and came to be revered as a martyr.
> Variants: Elphicke, Elfick, Elvidge, Alphege

Bardsley's *Dictionary of English and Welsh Surnames with Special American Instances* (1901) includes the surname Elphick with variants Elphic, Elphicke and Elfick:

> Baptismal name 'the son of Ælfech'. Mr Lower says, 'Ælfech occurs in Domesday as having been a sub-tenant in Sussex, *temp* Edward the Confessor, and not long previously (1006) St Elphegus or Alphage was archbishop of Canterbury'. This derivation seems natural.

> 1580   John Aynscombe and Susanna Elfeck, widow
>   *Allegations for Marriage Licences issued by the*
>   *Bishop of London* Geo J Armytage
> 1649   Margaret Elphick of Prescot
>   J P Earwaker FSA, *Wills at Chester* 1545-1720

1656   Robert Elphicke, St Dionis Backchurch,
        London J Lemuel Chester *St Dionis,*
        Backchurch, London 1538-1754
1667   John Elthicke and Mary Atkins married St
        James Clerkenwell, Robert Hovenden *St James,*
        Clerkenwell 1551-1754

London Commercial Directory 1870
Elphick   2
Elfick   2

Modern Domesday Book (Return of Owners of Land) –
county Essex
Elphic   1
Elphicke   1

Bardsley's examples include the variants Elfeck and
Elthicke. Our searches in census records located one
Elthick [*sic*] family in the 1881 census of Yorkshire (see
below), but no appearances of the name as Elthicke or
Elthick were found in any other census index or indeed
any other record consulted during this research.

Bardsley also listed how many occurrences of the
surname appeared in various directories he consulted.
In a commercial directory of London for 1870, he found
only two instances of the name as Elphick and two as
Elfick. He also consulted the *Return of Owners of Land*
(1873), commonly known as the Modern Domesday
Book (see below), in which he found Elphic and
Elphicke in Essex. His searches in these additional
sources do not appear to have located any other
occurrences of the name as Elthick(e).

C M Matheson in his *English Surnames* (1966) suggests that Affick might be another relative of the name Elphick, deriving from the Old English personal name *Ælfhēah*. Reaney and Wilson do not mention Affick, nor do Hank and Hodges. We did not find any examples of this possible variant during this research. Bardsley does not mention Affick but deals with the name Afflick in his *Dictionary of English and Welsh Surnames with Special American Instances* (1901). He states that this name is a variant of Affleck and that they are local names taken from a contraction of the name Auchinleck, which was the surname of an ancient Ayrshire family.

M A Lower's *Patronymica Brittanica* (1860), an early but still valuable surname dictionary, has been referred to above. Lower had a different etymological theory for the surname Elphick:

> **Elphick.** There is a group of names which may fairly be placed around this as a common centre; *viz* Alpha, Alphen, Alphew, Alpheg, Elphee, Elfeck, Alphegh *etc.* Ælfech occurs in Domes[day] as having been a sub-tenant in Sussex, *temp* Edw[ard] [the] Confessor, and not long previously, *viz* AD 1006, St Elphegus or Alphage was Archbishop of Canterbury. The personal name is evidently of A[nglo]-Sax[on] origin, and it has been derived from two words in that language – *al*, all, and *fegan*, to fix or join, and interpreted to signify 'a man who can do anything; a Jack of all Trades'.

Distribution

The existing volumes of the English Surname Series (which is very incomplete) have been consulted. In the volume dealing with the surnames of the West Riding of Yorkshire, George Redmonds does not mention Elphick but mentions the names Elvidge, Elwiss and Elviss. Redmond found all three names in south Yorkshire and states that the confusion between the two endings (-idge and -is(s)) is common in that area, citing as another example the names Wastnes and Wastnage. If we refer to Reaney's discussion of Alphege *etc* (see above) we can see that he included Margaret Elvishe (Yorkshire Wills 1609) as an example of the name. Unlike Redmonds, Reaney assumed a separate origin for Elwes, Elwess, Elwis, from the Old German word *Heilwidis* or *Helewidis* meaning 'hale or sound-wide'. The surname Elvidge would appear to be peculiar to the north of England and our limited research appears to confirm that this is the case. This suggests that the name has evolved differently in the north and south of England.

Richard McKinley's *Surnames of Sussex* (1988, page 434) cites Elphick as one of several surnames found in an 1850 directory of Brighton, of which he says that despite the influx of 'new' surnames over the years:

> Many of the more frequently found surnames at Brighton [in the 1850 directory] were ones which had a long history in Sussex, many of them ones to be found in the county during the 13th and 14th centuries, and many of them names which had probably arisen in the county.

In a slightly later work (*A History of British Surnames,* 1990), McKinley mentions Elphick again (page 96) as an example of a surname which survives today, and which was derived from a personal name that is now obsolete. He also describes it (page 106) as common in the south east of England (Kent, Surrey, Susses, Hampshire and Berkshire) before about 1500.

We consulted H R Moulton's *Palaeography, Genealogy and Topography,* which is primarily a sale catalogue printed in the 1930s. In here, there are listed historical documents, ancient charters, leases, court rolls etc., and this volume is a generally a good source for early examples of surnames. However, we found nothing for the name Elphick *etc* in Moulton and so we next consulted the online catalogue, *Access to Archives* (since replaced by the National Archives *Discovery Catalogue*). This is a consolidated index to the holdings of record offices and other archives throughout England which is constantly being updated. A check of this index found nothing for the surnames Affick, Alphegh, Alphege, Elfeck, Elthick or Elthicke. We noted the following entries for Elfick:

> **Extracts from a Survey of the Manor of Sandore-Sutton**
> Reference: SAS-M/1/356
> Date: 1565
> Made in the presence of John Hawes, gent., Thomas Taylor, Hughe Elfick, Thomas Elfick, Rich. Elfick, John Constable and Thomas Elfick, junr. and notes thereon

West Kent Quarter Sessions Records Recognizances
Reference: QM/SRc/1602/42
Dated 16 March 1601/2
Mark Jefferye of Hackington, labourer, in £13 6s. 8d. to appear, answer and to be of good behaviour; sureties, John Sebrand of St. Andrew's, Canterbury and John Elfick of the same, grocer

Charleston in Firle
Bargain and sale for £1800
Reference: SAS/G4/77
Date: 17 Nov 1614
John Lunsford of Wylygh in East Hothley, kt, his son and heir Thomas Lunsford, esq, and his wife Katharine, Anthony Apsley of Ticehurst, esq, and his wife Judith, and Cicely, one of the daughters of JL, to Thomas Elfick of Seaford, gent, and his son and heir Thomas Elficke

Berwick, Arlington
Copy of court roll, manor of Berwick
Reference: SAS/G41/54
Date: 1 Jun 1618
Surrender by Offington Elfick and re-grant according to the terms of SAS/G41/53 Thomas Whatman, steward, 1621

Counterpart of Deed of Feoffment
Reference: SAS-BB/66
Date: 22 Apr 1619
And the parsonage of Alfriston with glebe lands, tithes and profits And lands called Ballards Down in Selmiston purchased of Thos. Elfick of Seaford, gent

Bond

Reference: ASH/4501/537

Date: 6 Apr 1633

By John Cressy of Cattesfeild, collyer, to Edmund Elfick of Penherst [?Penshurst], husbandman, in £30 for good title &c. to 3 roods of land with a house in Penherst granted by the said John Crossy to the said Edmund by deed of even date. Signature and seal torn off

Bargain and Sale

Reference: ASH/4501/605

Date: 8 Jan 1640

Also the Hammerwood, 3 ac.; the Hammer brooke, 12 ac.; the Hammer hill and the Comes, 9 ac.; and 4 ac. formerly parcel of Hammerwood in the occupation of George Rabbett; the Upper Brook next the mill, the middle brooke next below the upper brooke and the brooke below the Middle Brooke, formerly part of the pond, containing 6 ac.; all in Ashbornham, bounding to the highway from Nenfeild to Ponts greene, N., a way from Ashborneham church to Kitchenham House, E., Thomas Luxford, gent., and William Moore, clerk, S. and lands of Thomas Elfick decd. and lands of George Thatcher, W

Miscellaneous Sussex Documents

Counterpart conveyance (bargain and sale) for £820

Reference: SAS/G35/28

Date: 15 Feb 1641

Thomas Gage, bt and his wife Mary, John Thetcher of Priesthawes [in Westham], esq, Augustine Belson of Brill, Buckinghamshire, esq, Edward Smith of Sandhill [in Framfield], esq and Thomas Roper of London, esq, to John Elfick of Clifford Inn, London, gent

Overseers of the Poor: settlement

Reference: PAR378/32/4/1

Settlement examinations

Date: 26 May 1748

Elizabeth Dan; born in East Hoathly; served Elizabeth Elfick of Chiddingly as a mantua maker, except for at hop-picking time; spent some time ill at her mother's home in East Hoathly; annotated with opinion of Henry Humphrey of Lewes, counsel, 30 May 1748

Deeds of the 'Rose and Crown Inn' Beckley

Reference: AMS5681/63

The will of Robert Elfick of Beckley victualler, dated June 1776 devised the 'Rose and Crown' alehouse and 3 acres of land to his son Thomas and daughter Elizabeth. John Freeland was a previous owner. In Oct 1792, this was sold for £460 to Thomas Coveney of Rolvenden (Kt) gent. (AMS5681/63/1-3) - the property had previously been called the May Pole and before that Poglas. In Jan 1795 it was sold for £500 to Samuel Baker of Beckley, yeoman (AMS5681/63/-8), who in turn sold it in Jun 1802 to William Collins the elder of Tenterden (Kt) yeoman (AMS5681/63/9)

William Collins - now described as of Northiam, yeoman, previously of Beckley, victualler sold the inn in Oct 1806 to Thomas Goland the elder of Udimore, yeoman (AMS5681/63/10-11). In Nov 1808, Goland sold the property to Edward Apps of Beckley, victualler for £770 (AMS5681/63/13-15). Apps also purchased a neighbouring messuage from Thomas Bowlin of Beckley, blacksmith in Jun 1820 (AMS5681/63/19-20): this had been built by Richard Elfick, yeoman and was subsequently owned by his son Thomas

HASTINGS
Deeds of properties near Tackleway, 1816 – 1953
Reference: HT 1067
Ebenezer House, 21 Woods Passage, All Saints
From a list of deeds convenanted to be produced, the property was conveyed by John Collier esq to Richard Cosens bricklayer, 10 & 11 Nov 1751. On 31 Dec 1768 Cosens & Sarah his wife mortgaged to John Elfick of Ninfield farmer and on 19 & 20 Dec 1776 sold to Thomas Kennard bricklayer & Thomas Dutton surgeon his trustee. Kennard sold to John Furner labourer & Edward Furner thatcher his trustee on 18 & 19 June 1812 & on 23 June the Furners mortgaged the property to Kennard for £200

The majority of these entries were from Sussex were the name was found as Elfick. As expected, when we used this index to check the names Elphick, Elphicke and Elvidge, there were a great many more entries. We extracted all pre-1700 references:

Access to Archives
The National Archives, online
Pre-1700 entries only:

Elphick	169 catalogue entries
Elphicke	33 catalogue entries
Elvidge	34 catalogue entries

Hamsey
Deed
Reference: SAS/PN/458
Date: 1 May 1560
Between John Sherman of Lewes, gent., of the one part and John Delve of Little Horsted, yeoman, Edward Browne of Southmalling, yeoman, and Bartylmewe Elphick of Baulsden, co. S Sussex,

yeoman, Overseers of the Will of John Brooke late of Ryngmere decd., of the other part, to lead the use of a Recovery to be suffered by the said John Sehrman - by way of Mortgage for £45 - to Johan Brooke and Alice Brooke, daughters and heirs of John Brooke, of a close called Brunesfelde containing 6 ac. in Hamsey, lying to lands of Edward Lewkwner, N., the said John Sherman, S., Risshely Common, W. and the highway from Cookes Bridge to Lewes, E. And also of another close containing 4 ac. in Hamsey lying to lands of Wm. Denham, N., the heirs of Thos. Beche, S., Rysshely Common, W. and the said Highway, E

Pevensey, &c
Demise (Not executed)
Reference: SAS-B/322
Date: 1588
And appointment of Edward Fylde of Battell, gent., and John Elphicke of Battell, yeoman, as attornies to give seisin

Fordwich Borough, Kent
Bundle No. 6 Miscellaneous.
Records of Court, Robt. Trytten v. Robt. Elvidge 1589.
Reference: U/4/6/125
Date: 1589

Corporation Estates
Feoffment (appointment of new trustees)
Reference: SEA/366
(i) Feoffment, 30 May 1592, by William Tipper and Robert Daw of London, gents., to John Row, sen., principal of Clifford's Inn, and Thomas Elphicke, sen., of Seaford, gent

Archive of Drake and Lee of Lewes, solicitor
Assignment - ref. SAS-D/77
Date: 25 Jun 1594
By William Wenmer of Heathefeld, co. Sussex, husbandman, to John Cosham of Heathfeld, husbandman, of a term of 1000 years granted by John Elphick of Heathfeld, yeoman, by deed dated 11 April, 38 Eliz., of 15 ac. of land late part of the lands of Tottingworth, upon which the said William had built a dwellinghouse and barn, lying in Heathfield to the rest of lands of John Elphick called Tottingworthe, W., S. and E., the common called Swyth corner being part of Heathfeld Downe, N. and W., one piece thereof being called the Mote of Tottingworth

Dobell family of Streat and Folkington, East Sussex
Lane family of Streat and Folkington, East Sussex
Westdene: Grant
Reference: SAS-M/1/488
Date: 3 Nov 1595
Witnesses to sealing and livery of seisin:--Edmund Elphicke, Thos Man, Roger Stroker

Corporation Estates
Reference: SEA/362
Date: c1595
Testimony signed by 18 inhabitants of Seaford as to the integrity of Thomas Elphicke, sen., jurat of Seaford, in purchasing the Common or Salts behalf of the town
WHEREAS it is of late given forth in speeches by some malycious and envious persons: And that not onlie to some gentlemen of good worshippe and callinge, but allso to Divers others that are of creditt. That Thomas Elphicke the elder of Seaforde within the countie of Sussex Juratt. Shoulde have bought and purchased the common or salts of Seaforde unto his owne proper Use his heirs and successors, by which

meanes hee should have injured and greatlie oppressed the poore of the same towne to their great hinderaunce and undoinge Soe it is that we the Freemen and Commoners of the saide Towne heareinge and understandinge that this our Neighboure shoulde be thus falslye and Unjustlie abused and the rather knowinge that both in regarde of his conscience towards god, and of his kindnesse and mercye towards the poore (as experience daylie sheweth) he never ment or intended any such wicked Acte, Doe thinke it meete and convenient as well for the avoidinge of all slaunders unjustlie objected against him, as allso for the discharging of our consciences who have manye yeares knowne the good and honest disposition of his life To make knowne to as manye as are desirous to knowe the truith of this matter and allso to declare his honest and charitable meaninge in purchasinge of the same

Wills and Inquisitions
Original will of John Gage of West Firle, esq
Reference: SAS/G7/12
date: 2 Jan 1596
W[itnesses]: Thomas Elffick, Edmund Elphick, Michael Okenden, John Duke, John Starte

Alciston Manor
Lease for 16 years at £6 13s 4d
Reference: SAS/G16/18
Date: 1 Sep 1596
Proviso for JG and the inhabitants in his mansion houses and messuages in Firle and Alciston to fell, coal and carry away as much of the said wood and underwood as required for fuel in the said houses; Edmund Elphick of Alciston to have 30 loads yearly for his house

Courts of Record and Assembly
Final Concords made in the Court of Record
Reference: SEA/36
Date: 14 March 1596/7
Before Thomas Elphicke, jun., bailiff, Thomas Elphicke, sen., and William Seger, jurats. Humphrey Rowe of Blatchington, pl. v. Richard Relphe of Northiam and w. Eleanor, def –

Deeds of Berwick, Selmeston and Ripe, 1663 – 1704
and of various parishes, 1597-1900
Probate (Letters missing) of the will of Seth Alcock of Midhurst, gent
Reference: AMS540
Date: 7 February 1600
To his wife Katherine, the rest of his goods and chattels unbequeathed and a lease of £5 p.a. for tithes paid by Edmond Elphick; in addition, all rents from lands and tenements, towards the upbringing of his children, and payment of legacies and debts until they come of age

Alciston Manor
Miscellaneous Documents
Proceedings by and against Edmund Elphick, lessee of the demesnes of Alciston, regarding tithes of the demesne lands
Reference: SAS/G16/81
Date: 1601-1628

Alciston Manor
Miscellaneous Documents
Pleadings in Richard Elphick v Edward Newton in common pleas in prohibition concerning the tithes Alciston
Reference: SAS/G16/82
date: 1603-1604

Hilary 1603; with drafts for an information in the court of common pleas by John Pyle of London, yeoman, against Thomas Dawson of Lewes, gent, for maintaining Elphick v Newton, Michaelmas 1604

Alciston Manor
Miscellaneous Documents
John Gage and Richard Elphick v Peter Smith, vicar of Alciston in exchequer concerning the tithes of the Alciston: draft bill and order
Reference: SAS/G16/83/9-10
Date: Feb 1605

Alciston Manor
Miscellaneous Documents
Information of Richard Elphick v Peter Smith in common pleas, Easter 1605
Reference: SAS/G16/83/11
Date: 1605

Court of Quarter Sessions
Precepts and Associated Documents
Reference: SEA/105
Date: 18 Oct 1608
Writ of distringas of Thomas Elphicke, jun., bailiff, to Thomas Jarvys, sergeant at mace, to empanel a jury to appear in a plea of trespass as in SEA/104 –

Miscellaneous Sussex Documents
Copy or draft defeasance of lease
Ref. SAS/G35/43
Date: 1 Feb 1613
John Gage of Firle, esq, and Robert Brooke of Frog Firle [in Alfriston], gent, Richard Elphicke of Alciston, yeoman, and Robert Alce of West Firle, yeoman

Draft Settlements Etc
Draft lease for 21 years at 20s
Reference: SAS/G39/4
Date: 1 Feb 1613
Marsh in two pieces called Locklands adjoining the way from Pevensey to Hooe in Pevensey Level; marsh called The Twenty Acres occupied by John Addams, shooting on the Locklands; [blank] Marsh or Fourteen Acres on the other side of the way; The Twelve Acres occupied by Michael Stert; Wylde Marsh; marsh occupied by Richard Elphicke adjoining the way from Pevensey to Hastings; Dongeon Salts, Great Dongeons, Little Dongeons and the Hundred Acres near Pevensey Haven; marshes occupied by Thomas Delves, gent, James Delves, gent, Thomas Tyndall, gent and Michael Sterte; the manor of Ersham or Hailsham

Draft Settlements etc
Lease for 21 years from 26 March 1613 at £10
Reference: SAS/G39/6A
Date: 15 Mar 1613
The manor of Eckington, the site of the manor of Ranscombe, the farm of Alciston occupied by Richard Elphicke and Alciston Coppice, messuages called Collyns, Myltons and the Lady Gage's houses and lands in Alciston occupied by James Rootes, gent, William Hersell and John Wheatley; the manors of Exceat and Friston, with land called Southcourte and Peveralls; land in Firle called The West Lease, The Myddle Lease, The East Lease, The Nether Rushett, The Upper Rushett, The Sharpride, and The Great Apterwell; lands occupied by John Coppley, before Thomas Pattricke, Robert Thornycrofte, John Orrell and John Ballarde; the site of the manor of Sholvestrode [in East Grinstead] and the demesne lands late in the tenure of Stephen Falconer, deceased

Firle
Charleston in Firle
Exemplification of common recovery
Reference: SAS/G4/78
Date: 7 Nov 1614
Thomas Elphicke, gent, against Anthony Apsley, esq of a messuage, dovehouse, garden, 110a of land, 20a of meadow and 176a of pasture in West Firle and Selmeston

Sussex Record Office – Miscellaneous
Exemplification of a verdict in exchequer in Hilary term 1577
Reference: SAS/A595
Date: 12 Feb 1614
Verdict upon an information exhibited by the Attorney General on behalf of the Queen against Edmund Elphick and Thomas Allen touching wreck of sea within the Manor of Bishopstone

Raper and Company, Solicitors, Chichester
Antiquarian Collection
Braban family of Mountfield and Salehurst Ockham House and Mill in Salehurst, purchased c1615
Counterpart pre-nuptial settlement (grant of £50 annuity)
Reference: AMS6227/7
Date: 29 Jul 1639
W[itnesses]: Thomas Elphicke, Thomas Ballowe

Berwick, Arlington
Partial enfranchisement for £80, manor of Berwick
Reference: SAS/G41/53
Date: 1 Jun 1618
Richard [Sackville], Earl of Dorset and his brother Edward Sackvill, kt, to Offington Elphicke of [East]Blatchington

*Deeds and Documents relating to lands formerly belonging
to the family of Fuller of Brightling Waldron*
Manor of Chittingligh
Reference: SAS-RF/2/6
Date: 20 Apr 1620
Copy of Court Roll of a Court of Sir Thos. Pelham,
bart., of a Conditional Surrender by John Barton To
the use of Richard Elphick of his assert land in
Waldron as security for £100

*Deeds and Documents relating to lands formerly belonging
to the family of Fuller of Brightling Waldron*
Manor of Laughton
Reference:. SAS-RF/2/7
Date: 4 Oct 1620
Copy of Court Roll of the Admission of Richard
Elphick under the above Surrender by John Barton to
12 acres of assert land and also land in Waldron
sometime Cavell's

*Deeds and Documents relating to lands formerly belonging
to the family of Fuller of Brightling Waldron*
Warbleton & Herstmonceux
Reference: SAS-RF/3
A messuage and 24 acres of land in Heathfield called
the Place of the Bache als Woodwards als Woodwools

Sutton and Seaford, Sussex
A Terrier of the manor of Sandore Sutton
Reference: SAS-M/1/380
Date: 1624
Belonging to Sir Benjamin Pellatt, knt., and the manor
of Michelham Sutton belonging to Thomas Elphick,
gent., with the lands of the tenants holding of these
manors and references to a Survey of this date (for
which see ESRO SEA 688) made by John Deward,
surveyor. Lands and furlongs mentioned:--

Winterlands, Merlins Pits, Croken Dyke, the Perry, Nore furlong, Langledean, Perrie furlong, the Lids, Havengate, Highland, Home furlong, Longwall furlong, Bramble furlong, Evengrove furlong, Shovel furlong, Gersland furlong, Bershall furlong, the Ham, Hales furlong, Silverlands alias Allands, Puckland furlong, Sandcliff furlong

Estate Maps
Survey of the manor of Sandore Sutton
Reference: SEA/688
Date: 1624
An exact and perfect Survey of ye Mannor of Sandore Sutton, parcell of ye Possessions of ye right worll Sr Beniamin Pellet knight, togither with ye Mannor of Michelham Sutton parcell of ye Possessions of Thomas Elphicke gent: wherein ye Mannor of Sandore Sutton is shadowed with yellow, ye Mannor of Michelham Sutton with Lake, ye Tenants Lands left white, and Nombers of reference are sett downe in each particuler parcell answerable to ye Booke of Survey thereof wherein is plainlye expressed ye quantities, qualities and all other remarkable things belonginge to this Plot of Survey. By Jo: De Ward, survayer, 1624. 20 in. to 1 m. 25 x 58½

Archive of Drake and Lee of Lewes, solicitor
Deed of feoffment
Reference: SAS-D/148
Date: 15 Sep 1625
Signature: Thomas Wekfford, tag.
Witnesses: Robert Hide, Richard Elphick

Ashburnham family of Ashburnham, East Sussex
Bargain and Sale
Reference: ASH/4501/497
Date: 25 Feb 1626
Witnesses to deed and livery of seisin:- John Elphicke
(X), Thos. French (X), William Wimble

Ashburnham family of Ashburnham, East Sussex
Deed
Reference: ASH/4501/503
Date: 5 May 1627
Witnesses:- Thos. Lee, Edward Collyns, Edward
Michell, Geo. Elphick, John Davies

Rye Harbour
Corporation Papers concerning Rye Harbour
Bond in £500 from Richard Luxford of Lewes, gent.,
to the mayor, etc., of Rye.
Reference: RYE/99/16
date: 27 February 1628
Witnesses: Thomas Elphicke, Jo. Lansdale, William
Gostrey.

Firle
Charleston in Firle
Counterpart settlement
Reference: SAS/G4/79
Date: 5 Feb 1629
Thomas Elphicke of Seaford, gent to William Thomas
of Westdean, gent, and his son and heir William
Thomas; Thomas Elphicke the younger to marry
William Thomas the elder's daughter Mary

Firle
Charleston in Firle
Counterpart settlement
Reference: SAS/G4/80
Date: 5 Feb 1629

Thomas Elphicke to William Thomas and his son William; Thomas Elficke the younger to marry William Thomas the elder's daughter Mary Thomas

Court in Session
Sessions Rolls
Presentment Roll
Presentment roll
Date: 1630-1
Reference: Q/SRp/m.8r [n.d.]
George Elphicke

Ashburnham family of Ashburnham, East Sussex
Bargain and Sale
Reference: ASH/4501/538
Date: 1 May 1633
Witnesses:- Gen. Scarlett, Geor. Elphick, Willm. Barley

Corporation Estates
Feoffment (appointment of new trustees)
Reference: SEA/366
(ii) Feoffment, 18 Aug. 1634, by John Row (as in (i)), to Sackvile Porter of Chinting in Seaford, esq. and his s. John, Thomas Elphicke, jun. of Seaford (grandson of Thomas Elphicke as in (i)), and s. William, Thomas Elphicke, sen. of Seaford, gent., and s. John, John Row, jun. of Lewes, gent., His Majesty's Customer of Sussex, and s. John
Witnesses to livery of seisin: Peter Card, bailiff; Thomas Harison, Stephen Elphicke, Thomas Beane, John Elphicke, Joshua Burdett, Henry Rose, Robert Raynes, John Swaine, John Hide, Francis Brodrick, John Tester, Simon Collingham, John Swaine, jun., Edward Goffe

Sussex
Eastbourne
Counterpart of Lease
Reference: SAS/PN/269
Date: 6 Aug 1634
By Henry Rogers of Selmeston, clerk, to John Elphicke of Eastebourne, yeoman, of a freehold messuage or tenement called Lampoortloate at Meadsey in the Burrough of Lampoort in Eastebourne and a barn thereunto adjoining and belonging, with the garden, yard, backside, close or fields belonging with arable or sowing lands belonging containing 34 ac., lying dispersed in several parcels in the common fields or laynes of the South part of Eastebourne and common of pasture for one ox on Grovedoune
Term, 21 years; rent, payable at Selmeston vicarage, £12. Signature, John Elphicke. Witnesses:- William Bishoppe, Richd. Whate (X), John Sharpe

Fragments
Reference: SEA/ 718
Dated: 3 Mar 1637/8
Fragment of a document, dated 3 March, 1637/8, signed by Thomas Elphicke, jun

Dobell family of Streat and Folkington, East Sussex
Lane family of Streat and Folkington, East Sussex
Westdean: Surrender
Reference: SAS-M/1/504
Date: 5 May 1641
Witnesses:--Thos. Elphicke, Edwd. Choune, Fran. Crompe

Ashburnham family of Ashburnham, East Sussex
Attested Copy of Will of Richard Weekes of Ashbornham, yeoman
Reference: ASH/4501/663
date: 21 May 1642

Nephews, John Botten, Richard Elphick, William Elphick, Robert Elphick, John Barker, Richard Barker, Nicholas Clevery, niece Joane Clevery

To brother William Weekes lands purchased of Thomas Byne either in the name of the testator or of the said William in "the Parishes" of Bulhurst and Catsfeild. Residuary legates and executor, nephew John Elphick

Hill Title
Miscellaneous Title
Sussex
Reference: D1229/1/7/32
Date: 12 November 1645
Quitclaim by Thomas Elphick and Samuel Fuller to Stephen French, of all their lands, tenements and woods called Pikely and the manor of Pasty Down in Chittingly and Hellingly.

[East] Blatchington, Eastbourne, Hailsham, Mountfield, Pevensey and Whatlington
Covenant to convey for £80
Reference: AMS5742/1
Date: 28 Mar 1646
Six pieces of land (6a) in the Long Deane; one piece (1a) in the Short Deane; three pieces (5a) in the Clinch; one acre bounding E[ast]: Thomas Elphicke gent's Winterland; N[orth]: RP's land; W[est]: Growdick; S[outh]: Thomas Seaman junior's land; one acre bounding N[orth]: Thomas Pelham bart's land; E[east]: RP's land; S[outh]: Richard Edborrowe's land; W[est]: Blatchington down common drove; two rods in Short Deane bounding N[orth]: Ward Downe; E[east]: Offington Elphicke's land; S[outh]: The Noore; W[est]: RP's land; ½a bounding N[orth]: The Noore; W[est]: Thomas Seaman junior's land; S[outh]: Offington Elphicke's 'Pereivall'; E[ast]: Robert

Adams' land; all in [East] Blatchington W[itnesses]:
William Alcock, Richard Isted

Stapley Family
Account book
Reference: HIC/467/12
Date: 1646
A1 "charges for sute with mr Thomas Elphick"

Ashburnham family of Ashburnham, East Sussex
Copy of Will of Bartholomew Jeffery of Battell,
yeoman
Reference: ASH/4501/645
Date: 30 Nov 1647
Elizabeth Elphick, daughter of Thos. Elphick of
Penhurst. Godson, Thos. Coberne of Wartlinge

Dobell family of Streat and Folkington, East Sussex
Lane family of Streat and Folkington, East Sussex
Westdean: Conveyance
Reference: SAS-M/1/681
Date: 17 Jul 1648
Signatures of Thomas Gage and Robert Pickering and
seals. Witnesses to sealing and livery of seisin:--Geo.
Elphicke, *t*enant of the premises, Tho. Hewes, William
Myner, Rose Woodyson

Firle
Charleston in Firle
Conveyance (bargain and sale) for £2550
Reference: SAS/G4/81
Date: 14 Jan 1648
Thomas Elphick of Seaford, gent to Walter Evernden
of Chinting [in Seaford], gent and Robert Pickering of
East Grinstead [in trust for Thomas Gage, bt]

Exceat in West Dean and Friston
Southcourt in Exceat
Conveyance (bargain and sale) for £45
Reference: SAS/G5/24A,B
Date: 14 Apr 1648
14a Of land in Exceat (E: land of WT; W,N,S: other lands of TG), occupied by George Elphick, gent

Firle
Charleston in Firle
Conveyance (bargain and sale) for £2550
Reference: SAS/G4/81 Date: 14 Jan 1648
Witnesses: William Thomas, William Wynde, Stephen Elphicke, Alexander Alchorne, Thomas Moore, Richard Alchorne

Estate of John Piper of East Hoathly
East Hoathly
Conveyance (feoffment with covenant to levy fine and recovery) for £200
Reference: AMS5923/18
Date: 29 Oct 1648
John Pope of Clifford's Inn gent and John Elphicke of London gent to be parties to the fine and recovery

Firle
Charleston in Firle
Mortgage for £2000
Reference: SAS/G4/82
Date: 15 Jan 1648
Walter Evernden and Robert Pickering to Thomas Elphicke, William Thomas and Anthony Fowle of Grays Inn, esq, of the manor of Charleston as SAS/G4/81

Miscellaneous Sussex Documents
Unexecuted settlement (deed poll)
Reference: SAS/G35/34
date: 1649
Recites: seisin of Walter Everden of Chinting [in
Seaford] and Robert Pickering of East Grinstead,
gents, of the manor of Charleston [in Firle], purchased
of Thomas Elphick, gent, and occupied by Alexander
Alchorne; seisin of TG and RP of marshland in
Pevensey

Ashburnham family of Ashburnham, East Sussex
Quit-claim
Reference: ASH/4501/653
Date: 13 Apr 1649
By John Tharpe of Nenfeild, butcher, and Mary his
wife, one of the daughters of John Weekes decd., to
Richard Weekes, brother of the said Mary, - in
consideration of £25 paid by John Elphicke of
Ashbornham, yeoman, executor of the will of Richard
Weekes late of Ashbornham decd., - of and in divers
lands and tenements in Cattesfeild and Penherst
which were granted by the said Richard Weekes decd.
to Elizabeth Weekes, widow, by deed dated 10 July,
15 Chas. I to the use of the 4 children of John Weeks to
be equally divided between them, with a proviso for
defeazance on payment by the said Richard to the
said 4 children of John Weekes, of whom the said
Mary is one, of £100 to be equally divided

Miscellaneous Sussex Documents
Unexecuted settlement (deed poll)
Reference: SAS/G35/34
Date: 1649
TG, in pursuance of powers reserved, appoints the
income from the rents or sale of the manors for the
payment of debts (annuity of £92 to Penelope Harvey;
£500 to Roger Gregory of Cookham in Oxfordshire,

gent; £600 to Danmiel Enderby of Staines in M[iddlese]x, tanner; £400 to Thomas Elphicke of Seaford, gent; £200 in debts to various persons owed by TG's wife Mary Gage); and raising £4000 for portions for his younger daughters

Ashburnham family of Ashburnham, East Sussex
Lease
Reference: ASH/4501/666
Date: 26 Mar 1649
By Elizabeth Weeks of Dallington, widow, to Richard Weekes of Nendfeild, yeoman, of the estate and thirds of the said Elizabeth, by the death of her husband Richard Weeks, of and in 15 ac. of land called Berglands and 1 ac. of wood adjoining in Nendfeild in the occupation of John Elphick Also Homefeild (7 ac.); part of Wyldwood (11 ac.); Herstwood (4 ac.); which premises were laid out as her thirds by the Under Sheriff of Sussex - the last mentioned premises being in Ashburnham in the occupation of John Elphick and James Cowper. Term, the life of the said Elizabeth, rent £8

Incumbent: registers
Pre-1812 registers
General register
Reference: PAR227/1/1/1
Date: 1575-1702
f25r note of baptisms performed by several ministers during a vacancy at Alciston - the children of William and Mary Elphicke, [blank] 1650 - Feb 1663, the children of John and Judith Cleaver, May 1641 - Mar 1655

Ashburnham family of Ashburnham, East Sussex
Bargain and Sale
Reference: ASH/4501/697
Date: 10 Jan 1652
Signature of John Gyles (only) Witnesses:- Richd. Ralfe, Wm. Coby, John Elphick

Wootton in Folkington
Mortgage
Reference: SAS-M/1/214
Date: 29 Jul 1653
Signatures of both parties. Witnesses:--Ben Scarlett, Richd. Adams, John Stapley, Richd. Elphick, Thos. Peachey

Ripe, Sussex
Bargain and Sale
Reference: SAS-M/1/271
date: 7 Jun 1653
By William Thomas of Westdene, esq., and Katharine his wife to Richard Acton of Chalvington, gent.--for £560--of 42 ac. of land, meadow and pasture ground called Sheepelands in Ripe alias Ekington, in the tenure of Thomas Elphick, gent
Witnesses:--George Elphick, Ben. Scarlett, John Caly

Title deeds: Farnden family
Deeds of the Manor of Crowham, Crowham forge, Conster forge and furnace in Brede
Copy settlement of 24 Aug 1653
Reference: DUN 27/2
Date: 8 Oct 1653
5 Messuage and land called Puster in Brede occupied by William Elphicke
6 12a arable and pasture in Beckley, occupied by William Elphicke

Raper and Company, Solicitors, Chichester
Antiquarian Collection
Quitclaim and receipt for £100
Reference: AMS6227/8
Date: 12 Nov 1655
W[itnesses]: John Elphicke, Anthony Becke, John Derbyshire

Ashburnham family of Ashburnham, East Sussex
Counterpart of Bargain and Sale
Reference: ASH/4501/730
Date: 23 Mar 1655
By Richard Weekes of Ashburnham, yeoman, and Mary his wife to Elizabeth Jefferie of Nendfield, widow, - for £111 - of 18 ac. called Burgland in Mendfield bounding to the highway leading from Burnt Barnes to Nendfield, N. and NW., land of Thos. Eason in part and land of Hugh Dulvie, E., land late of John Gyles, clerk, in part and John Elphick in part, S. and W

Deeds of Charity Farm, Chiddingly
Assignment of mortgage (feoffment) for £280 with counterpart
Reference: AMS6013/1,2
Date: 6 April 1657
John Elphicke of Chiddingly, yeoman and Richard Browne of Waldron, yeoman, to Stephen Frenche of Chiddingly esq
Hotchingdowne, Welldowne, the Four Acres and Pickentemere; E: Thunderhill-Horam road; S: Warnefoulds Cross - Chiddingly Mill lane; SW: Thomas Jefferay esq; W,N: JE Cookes: W: lane above; E: late Richard Elphicke; S: The Stroode; S,W: Thomas Jefferay esq.

The Cinque Ports
Clerk of the Brotherhood
Reference: NR/CPc/172
Dated 24 July 1660
Petition of Stephen Elphick, bailiff of Seaford to the
Guestling.

Archive of the Fuller-Acland-Hood family, Barons St Audries
Premises in Westham and Hailsham
Reference: SAU/1018-1041
Date: 1664-1722

In 1664 Edward Peake of Westham, gent., mortgaged
the premises (i) to Henry Bill of Lewes, gent., and in
1665 he made another mortgage of the premises to
Richard Store of Wilmington, yeo. Henry Bill
assigned his mortgage to Richard Store in 1668.
No.SAU/1025, 1686, is an agreement between William
Adams of Wilmington, yeo., and w. Dorothy, Anne
Store of Wilmington, spinster, Mary Store of
Wilmington, spinster, and Edmund Elphicke of
Westdean, yeo. (Dorothy, Ann and Mary were
daughters and ex'ors of Richard Store of Wilmington,
dec'd.). A farm and barn called the Monte (45a.) in
Folkington was to go to William Adams and w.
Dorothy; Ann Store was to have the Seven Acre field,
part of Monte Farm in Folkington and the premises (i)
in Westham; Mary Store was to have 13a. marsh
called Unsteds Wall in Hailsham, and field called
Upper Six Acres, part of Monte Farm in Folkington. In
1690 Anne Store mortgaged the premises to Thomas
Tourle of Lewes, butcher, and this was assigned to
Benjamin White of Lewes, Dr. in Physic, in 1690. No.
SAU/1033, is the letters of administration of Ann
Store, issued at Lewes 1700. In 1702 Benjamin White
bought the premises (i) from Arthur Brook of
Lullington, yeo., and w. Charity, Benjamin Austen of
Burwash, mercer, and w. Katherine, William

Blackman of Wilmington, yeo., and w. Mary, John Hicks, jun., of Burwash, yeo., and w. Elizabeth (Charity, Katherine, Mary and Elizabeth were sisters of Ann Store, dec'd). In 1703 John Peake of Westham confirmed the sale to Benjamin White

Wolryche family of Bridgnorth
Muniments of Title
Family Settlements and related papers
Deed to declare the uses of a fine (endorsed: revoked)
Reference: 2922/3/38
Date: 13 January 1663/4
£1100 to Anthony Windsor, Worcester; £200 to Geo Elphicke, Greys Inn

Dobell family of Streat and Folkington, East Sussex
Lane family of Streat and Folkington, East Sussex
Counterpart of Lease
Reference: SAS-D/259
Date: 12 Apr 1664
Witnesses:- John Elphicke, Robert Raynes

Sussex Record Office – Miscellaneous
Lease for a year
Reference: SAS-RF/13/27
Date: 30 Aug 1664
By Richard Glyd senr. of Blechingley, Surrey, gent, to Richard Chandler, citizen and haberdasher of London, William Wright, citizen and clothworker of London, and John Elphick and Michael Glyd of London, gents.

Court in Session
East Kent
Order Book
East Kent Order Book, Midsummer 1664 –
Reference: Q/SO/E1/f.91 [n.d.]

The like order for Richard Elphicke and Henry
Reeves, inhabitants of Wittersham.

Winton Farm in Alfriston and Berwick
Conveyance for £221, with bond
Reference: SAS/G29/9-10
Date: 12 Oct 1666
Robert Haffenden of Tenterden, Kent, gent, and his
wife Margaret and John Elphick of Eastbourne,
mercer, and his wife Elizabeth to John Brooke of
Alfriston, gent

Ashburnham family of Ashburnham, East Sussex
Lease for a year
Reference: ASH/4501/845
Date: 22 Jun 1666
By Sir Charles Colbrond of Tunbridge, co. Kent, bart.,
to John Elphick of Cliffords Inn, London, gent., of 87
ac. of marshland called Southleas in the occupation of
Richard Day and Thomas Day of Mayfeild, lying in
Westham and Pevensey. Signature, Charles Colbrond,
and covered seal

Ashburnham family of Ashburnham, East Sussex
Grant
Reference: ASH/4501/846
date: 22 Jun 1666
By Sir Charles Colbrond to John Elphick of the same
premises

Ashburnham family of Ashburnham, East Sussex
Release
Reference: ASH/4501/847
Date: 23 Jun 1666
By Sir Charles Colbrond to John Elphick of the
marshlands described in Lease for a year - for £830

Ashburnham family of Ashburnham, East Sussex
Bond
Reference: ASH/4501/848
date: 23 Jun 1666
By Sir Charles Colbrond to John Elphick for performance of covenants

Ashburnham family of Ashburnham, East Sussex
Lease for a year
Reference: ASH/4501/849
date: 8 Aug 1666
By John Elphick of Cliffords Inn, London, gent., to Arthur Amherst of Tonbridge, co. Kent, doctor in physick, of the marshlands described in deeds of 22 and 23 June, 1666

Ashburnham family of Ashburnham, East Sussex
Deed
Reference: ASH/4501/864
date: 23 Oct 1667
Between Sir Charles Colbrond of Tonbridge, co. Kent, bart., and Arthur Amherst of Tunbridge, doctor in physick, and John Hooper of St Andrew's, Holborne, co. Middlesex, gent. - for confirming the title of the said Arthur Amherst in the marshlands mentioned and already conveyed to him by John Elphick, and for £700 paid to the said Sir Charles Colbrond - to lead the use of a Fine of

Sutton and Seaford, Sussex
A Rental of Sandore Sutton
Reference: SAS-M/1/382
Date: 7 Oct 1667
Tenants named:--Freeholders: Heirs of Thos. Elphick, gent., Thos. Harrison, gent., Thos. Becke, the heirs of William Jeffery, Nicholas Selwyn in right of his wife, Thos. Bean, gent.--Copyholder: Nichs. Selwyn. Total

rents:-- 8s. 0¾d. Other lands holden of the manor, but rents long discontinued. Richard Isted, steward

Wolryche family of Bridgnorth
Deed to declare the uses of a fine
Reference: 2922/3/39
Date: 23 April 1667
(2) John Wolryche of Greys Inn, son of Sir Thomas George Elphicke of Greys Inn

Winton Farm in Alfriston and Berwick
Copy of court roll, manor of Berwick
Reference: SAS/G29/12
Date: 28 Aug 1667
1 8a At Weeke Street in Arlington late John Elphicke, sometime Edward Walker, quitrent 2s 1d

Wolryche family of Bridgnorth
Lease and release (docketed: Last Settlement of Sir Tho. Wolryche)
Reference: 2922/3/42-43
Date: 17 & 18 April 1668
For assuring the property below and for Sir Thomas's love for Francis, William, Thomas and John Wolryche his sons, and for payment of Sir Thomas's debts mentioned in the schedule annexed, and of the portions appointed to be paid to the younger daughters of Sir Thomas, Sir Thomas grants to John Wolryche all his manors and property in Dudmaston, Wroxeter, Hughley, Quatt, Quatt Malver and Quatt Jervis, Brompton, Much Wenlock, Presthope, Berrington, Uppington, Donnington and Leighton, Whitley Fields in Cleverley, houses in Shrewsbury, and Quatford weir, to be held on trust:- that William and Thomas Wolryche should have the residue of the manors and lands; that Francis Wolryche should receive £50 p.a. out of the rents, and that Sir Thomas's debts should be paid, and that £2000 should be paid

to William Wolryche and that he should receive lands to the value of £200 p.a. on his marriage; that 1000 marks should be paid to Susanna and Elizabeth Wolryche; that £1150 be paid to Anthony Windsor of Worcester; and £200 to Mary Elphicke.

Overseers of the Poor
Apprenticeship indenture of Edmund Daw, an orphan
Reference: PAR375/33/1
Date: 2 Aug 1669
John Elphick and Thomas Browne (churchwardens), John Pettett and John Parris (overseers) with the consent of Sir John Pelham bt and Sir Thomas Dyke kt to George Daw of Bexhill yeoman and wife Ann, for £10; Edmund Daw, an orphan, apprenticed in husbandry until the age of 24

Membership of the Cinque Ports
Reference: SEA/401
Date: 1669-1670
Note of expenses, £32. 2s. 7d., incurred by Stephen Elphicke, bailiff, and the Corporation of Seaford in connexion with a lawsuit between Sir John Gage and certain inhabitants of Seaford for fishing in Cuckmere

Courts of Record and Assembly
Final Concords made in the Court of Record
Reference: SEA/37
Date: 16 Jan 1670/1
Before Stephen Elphicke, esq., bailiff, Thomas Beane, Robert Howell and Henry Wymarke, jurats. Philip Taverner, pl., v. Edward Rance and w. Susanna, def –

Sussex Record Office - Miscellaneous
Lease for a year
Reference: SAS-RF/13/30
Date: 2 Mar 1671

By Richard Chandler, William Wright, John Elphick and Michael Glyd to Nicholas Stoughton, bart., and Anne Glyd of Blechingley, widow, late the wife of Richard Glyd junr. decd., of the said woods in Brightling (described as before)

Fines and Recoveries
Reference: SAS/G2/18
date: Easter term 1672
Fine - Walter Evernden and Robert Pickering, querents, and Thomas Elphick and his wife Mary, deforciants, of lands in West Firle and Selmeston and 1 messuage, 1 dovehouse, 1 garden, 110a of land, 20a of meadow and 176a of pasture in West Firle and Selmeston

Sussex Deeds
Deeds of 44 High Street, Lewes, 1672 – 1912
Reference: AMS5742
On 1 May 1672 William Alcocke of Lewes gentleman bequeathed a tenement (occupied by William Elphicke, William Marshall and Richard Mantle) which he had purchased from Samuel Towers to his youngest daughter Mary wife of William Pellatt gentleman along with other property, including The Friars, Lewes, and Old Malling. The will was proved in 1694 in PCC and on 22 June 1695 Pellatt (now citizen and ironmonger of London) settled the property as a jointure for his wife with remainder to their son William who himself (then of Penhill in Bletchingly Surrey Esq) settled it on his marriage with Katherine sister of Henry and Leonard Gale of Worth, 23 July 1701; the property was then described as 4 houses, buildings and land (3a) occupied by Thomas Barrett, widow Elphick, William Rose and another. On 30 Nov 1727 Katherine Pellatt now a widow and her son Leonard P of London merchant mortgaged the property (occupied by Robert Walter and

undertenants at a total rent of £30) to Leonard Gale; a recovery was also suffered to bar the entail created by the 1701 settlement. When on 10 Aug 1733 Leonard Pellatt reconveyed his reversion of the jointure estate (still mortgaged) to his mother it was stated that the mortgage was to enable him to carry on business. By her will of 16 Nov 1752 Katherine Pellatt of West Grinstead widow made her daughter Philippa residuary legatee and she by her will of 21 Sep 1753 devised the property to her cousin Henry Woodward rector of West Grinstead

Correspondence - Jeake and associated families
Letters to Samuel Jeake the elder (1623-1690)
Letter from William Elphicke, Lewes on legal matters
Reference: FRE/4666
Date: 4 Feb 1673
Letter from William Elphicke, Lewes concerning Pierre Boytoult
Reference: FRE/4722
Date: 4 Nov 1673

Estate of Joseph Fuller of Arlington and Selmeston
Selmeston: Pre-nuptial settlement (lease and release)
Reference: AMS5923/11, 12
Date: 29 and 30 Sept 1673
2. The Pight (10½a) occupied by William Elphicke

Cobb Place Estate in Beddingham
Conveyance for £300
Reference: SAS/G22/60
date: 17 Jun 1674
Witnesses: Henry Shelley, Thomas Pellatt, Stephen Elphicke

Ecclesiastical and Parish Records
Rectory of Beddingham
Lease for lives at an annual rent of £20 6s. 8d. from George Stradling, D.D., Dean of Chichester and the Chapter of Chichester to (b) Thomas Pellet of Lewes, gent.
Reference: GLY/3395
Date: 13 October 1674
Witnesses: William Winton, Richard Elphicke.

Muniments of Title
Reference: ACC/0446/ED/267
Harlington
Date: 1675
Round Close (7a.), Windsor Close and Little Pightell. Assignment of Lease from 1 to 3. –
1. John Elphicke
2. Thomas Elphicke.

Corporation Estates
Feoffment (appointment of new trustees)
Reference: SEA/366
Date: 1 May 1675
John Row of Hurst, woollen-draper (s. and h. of John Row who was s. and h. of John Row of Lewes His Majesty's Customer of Sussex who was s. and h. of John Row, sen. of Lewes, gent., principal of Clifford's Inn, London), to Peter Gard of Seaford, gent. and bailiff of Seaford, Thomas Harison, Stephen Elphicke, Thomas Beane, Robert Howell and Henry Wymarcke, all jurats and freemen of Seaford, Thomas Elphicke of London, citizen and grocer, Thomas Elphicke of Seaford (nephew of the said Stephen Elphicke), and John Harison of Seaford (son of the said Thomas Harison)

Cobb Place Estate in Beddingham
Exemplification of common recovery
Reference: SAS/G22/75
Date: 28 May 1677
Richard Isted, gent, against Thomas Isted, gent, with Richard Elphick as vouchee, of 10a of fresh marsh in Beddingham

Berwick
Settlement (deed to lead the use of a fine)
Reference: SAS/G40/137
Date: 1 May 1678
2 A messuage or cottage and ½a called Austens (E: the Tye of Berwick; S: The Sawyers; W: other land of GN; N: land of Nathaniel Elphick)

Ringmer
Mortgage
Reference: SAS/PN/627
Date: 20 Dec 1680
By John Delves of Vuggles in Newick, gent., to Thomas Medley of Barcombe, gent. - for £100 - of a messuage, barn, orchard, garden and close containing 1 ac. in the Borough of Norlington in Ringmer adjoining to the Broyle, S. and N., to lands of Richard Elphick, W. and lands late of John Beecher, E. Also of and in a parcel of meadowland called Sheerewish, containing 3 ac. in the said borough of Norlington adjoining to lands of John Spence, esq., called Potters, S. and lands of Thos. Mathew, N.; the premises being then in the tenure of John Foord senr

Mocketts in West Firle
Conveyance (feoffment) for £900
Reference: SAS/G25/1
Date: 1 Mar 1681
Stephen Elphicke of Seaford, gent, attorney to deliver seisin

Pelham family, Earls of Chichester, of Stanmer, Sussex
Copy probate (PCC) of the will (9 Jan 1682) of Robert
Heath of Lewes, esq
Reference: SAS/A246
Date: 23 May 1682
Contingent remainders severally to cousin Henry
Shelley of Lewes, esq, cousin Thomas Shelley of
Lewes, gent, cousin Edward Bray of Surrey, gent,
Aunt Elphick (wife of Stephen Elphick of Seaford,
gent) for life, remainder to William Dobyng of
Lincoln's Inn in trust for cousin Mary Jenkins
(daughter of Aunt Elphick)

Dobell family of Streat and Folkington, East Sussex
Lane family of Streat and Folkington, East Sussex
Assignment
Reference: SAS-D/418
Date: 10 Jun 1682
By Richard Read of Ringmer, co. Sussex, yeoman - by
direction of Thomas Harrison of Sutton, co. Sussex,
gent. - to Thomas Shelley of Lewes, gent., as trustee
for Stephen Elphicke of Seaford, gent., of a Mortgage
dated 24 April, 27 Chas. II, by the said Thomas
Harrison and others to the said Richard Read - for
£450 - of (amongst other lands) a piece of meadow
called the Gore containing 20 ac. in Seaford and
Sutton, which the said Stephen Elphicke lately
purchased of the said Thos. Harrison and John
Harrison his eldest son

Deeds and Documents relating to lands formerly belonging
to the family of Fuller of Brightling Waldron
Deed of feoffment
Reference: SAS-RF/3/72
date: 15 Nov 1682
By Thomas Thorpe, Edmund Thorpe and John Thorpe
to Thomas Crouch of the premises described in

Bargain and Sale of even date (SAS-RF/3/69). Witnesses to livery of seisin on 6 Dec. 1682, by John Cruttenden as attorney:- Joseph Weller, Henry Cruttenden, Thomas Elphick (X)

Berwick
Lease for 1000 years at a nominal rent for £10 12s
Reference: SAS/G40/138
Date: 18 Feb 1684
Witnesses: William Nowell, Edmund Elphicke, William Hoder

Miscellaneous Documents
Quitclaim (unexecuted)
Reference: SEA/698
Date: 8 July 1686
1a. abutting W. on lands late of Roger Gratwicke, dec'd, near Crouch Lane, and E. on lands late of Thomas Elphick, jun., dec'd, near Hangmans Acre; 2½a. lying at the E. end of Graseland Furlonge; 1a. in the said Furlong abutting N. on lands late of Roger Gratwicke; 2r. in the said Furlong abutting N. and W. on lands of Sir William Thomas, and E. on lands late of Roger Gratwicke; ½a. in the Home Furlonge and lately enclosed by the said Peter Gard with a wall and pale. All in Sutton and Seaford, and late in the occ. of the said Peter Gard and John Mullett dec'd, and now in the occ. of John Gaston

Southerham in South Malling
Southerham Prebend
Probate (Lewes) of the will (4 Nov 1685) of Elizabeth Alcock of Lewes, widow
Reference: SAS/G34/88
date: 1 Jun 1686
To executrixes in trust for sale for performance of will, all freehold and copyhold messuages and land held of the manor of Ranscombe in South Malling and

at Southerham and the moiety of the prebendary rectory or parsonage of Southerham, with all tithes late Charity Storer, and a copyhold messuage and land in Beddingham late Richard Elphick deceased

Archive of Drake and Lee of Lewes, solicitor
Bargain and Sale
Reference: SAS-D/428
Date: 8 Nov 1686
Signatures of Francis Brotherick, Thos. Sargent and Mary Sargent.
Witnesses to deed and livery of seisin:- Nichs. Dobson, Stephen Elphick, John Hide, Tho. Willard

Archive of Drake and Lee of Lewes, solicitor
Fine in the King's Court at Seaford
Reference: SAS-D/430
Date: 9 Nov 1686
Before Nicholas Dobson, esq., Stephen Elphick, gent., John Hide, gent., and John Harrison, gent., Jurats, between Henry Knight, querent, and Francis Brotherick and Thomas Serjeant and Mary his wife, deforciants, of a messuage and a parcel of land containing 75 ft. by 60 ft. in Seaford. Tho. Willard, bailiff

General Estate Archives
Reference: LAVINGTON/55
Date: 11 Feb 1686/7
Account of rent payable, after deductions, by Walter Elphick to Francis Holroyd for land at Duncton. Receipted by John Dee. -

Estate Archives
Blatchington Manor
Reference: SAS-DR/29
Date: 25 Apr 1688

Surrender by Thomas Elphick to the use of his Will of 24 ac. called Tarrie and 20 ac. called Percival Dibbe.

Deeds of various parishes
Conveyance (lease and release) Consideration £5
Reference: Add Mss 8756
Date: 4 February 1689/90
(a) Nathaniel Palmer as in Add Mss 8755, to (b) Walter Elphicke of Petworth, gent

Court Rolls and Associated Papers
Sussex
Reference: PHA/3141
Date: 10 Sept 1690
Duncton. Surrender of tenement called Mannings, with other lands, by John Ford, William Twyne and Richard Hale to Walter Elphick of Rotherbridge in Petworth and John Poleing of Fittleworth as security for £82 borrowed by John Ford.

Title Deeds
The Crabbett Estate in Worth, Crawley, Ifield and Slaugham - Conveyance (lease and release)
Reference: LYTTON/207-210 -
Date: 17, 18 March 1692/3
with counterpart of release and bond. Consideration: an annuity of £70; Henry Stiles, of West Tarring, gent. to Walter Elphick, of Petworth, gent. and John Groomes, of Steyning, gent.
Witnesses: John Newton, Alice Elphick, and John Alcock, jun.

Blatchington Manor
Conditional Surrender by Thomas Elphicke to the use of Ann Barnham of Selmeston, of a barn and 24 ac. called Tarres and 20 ac. called Percival Dibbs inoccupation of John Dippery –
Reference: SAS-DR/33; Date: 2 Oct 1693

House of Lords: Parliament Office: Journal Office
House of Lords: Journal Office: Main Papers 1509-1700
Main Papers 675 – 687
Petworth (North Chappell, &c.) Act
Reference: HL/PO/JO/10/1/454/676
Date: 27 Jan 1693
Consent of parishioners of Petworth, in Vestry assembled, to the passing of the Bill "for dividing the Chapelries of North Chappell and Dungton from the parish of Petworth, and erecting them into new parishes; and for settling the Advowsons and rights of Patronage of the Rectories of Petworth, North Chappell, Dungton, Clewer, Farnham Royall, Worplesdon, Kirby Overblowes, and Catton, and the Vicarage of Long Horsley," so far as the Bill relates to the proposed new parish of Dungton. Signed by John Cook, Will. Peachey. Henry Barnard, John Dee, Hen. Bulstrode, Francis Mose, Humph, Tewkes, Rich. Stills, Francis Mose, junr., Walter Elphicke, Tho. Moody, Jonathan Harris, Thomas Coward, Jeffery Dawtrey, Richard Taylor, Richard Browne, George Finch, William Kelmes (by his mark), Thomas Smart, Peter Valler, James Dawtrey, James Smart, Thomas Hughes, Henry Damer, and John Atkinson. Dated 6 Nov 1692. Endorsed Duke of Somerset.

Court in Session
Sessions Papers.
Reference: Q/SB/24/165
Date: 1694-97
Letter from the vicar and parish officers of Ticehurst, Sussex, to [?Robert Saunders] that the recognizance of William Pierce of Goudhurst for begetting a bastard child on the body of Elizabeth Elphick of Ticehurst, should be withdrawn as he has given satisfaction to the parish

Premises in Malling Street, Lewes, formerly called Copped Hall; 1675 to 1864
Assignment of same Term for £10
Reference: SAS-BR/342
date: 2 Nov 1696
Thomas Ince, of Chalvington als Chaunton, husbandman, to Edward Elphicke, of Chiddingly, butcher

Premises in Malling Street, Lewes, formerly called Copped Hall; 1675 to 1864
Deed Poll of Assignment of same Term
Reference: SAS-BR/343
date: 15 Apr 1698
Anne Parkes, of Waldron, w[i]d[ow], a d[augh]t[e]r & co-heiress of Tho Bennett, late of Hellingly, yeo[man], to Edw Elphicke

Blatchington Manor
Conditional Surrender by Thomas Elphicke to the use of Ann Barnham of lands called Tarres and Persival Dibbs
Reference: SAS-DR/37
Date: 2 Oct 1698

Arlington
Lease for a year
Reference: SAS-N/467
Date: 11 Jan 1698
By Thomas Frewen of Northiam, esq., eldest son of Thomas Frewen late of Northiam, clerk, to Thomas Weston of Cranbrooke, Kent, gent., of the messuage or tenement called Stacys in Arlington with lands &c. containing 120 ac., theretofore in the occupation of Thomas Reada and then of Gerrard Mason and George Beard and bounding to the king's highway from Berwick Common to the Dicker, W. and to lands

theretofore of John Elphick, S. and lands theretofore of Laurence Piers, esq., E. and to a lane, N.a nd E.
Signature of lessor and armorial seal

Premises in Malling Street, Lewes, formerly called Copped Hall; 1675 to 1864
Assignment of same Term for £23-15-0
Reference: SAS-BR/344
Date: 10 May 1698
Edward Elphick to Robert Hammond the younger, of Lewes, gt

Archive of Drake and Lee of Lewes, solicitor
Mortgage
Reference: SAS-D/490
Date: 20 Oct 1699
By Thomas Elphick of Seaford, co. Sussex, gent., nephew and heir of Stephen Elphick late of the same place, gent. deceased, to Thomas Willard of Eastbourne, gent., - for £100 - of a piece of land called the Gore and Gorefeild containing 20 ac. in Seaford and Sutton in the occupation of the said Thos. Elphick and late the lands of the said Thomas (sic) Elphick deceased, bounding to Seaford Down, S., the Downe and arable of the said Down and Seaford Brooks, S. and W., lands of Sir William Thomas called Sandore, E. and other lands of Sir Wm. Thomas belonging to his manor of Sutton Sandore and lands belonging to the manor of Michelham Sutton called the Westernham and the Middleham...
Signature, Thos. Elphick, and seal.
Witnesses:- Fran. Green, Lod. Wilson

Hamsey
Lease for a year
Reference: SAS/PN/489
Date: 16 Oct 1699
Witnesses:- Tho. Medley, John Elphick, Elyott
Richbell

Overseers of the Poor
Settlement
Removal order from Chiddingly
Reference: PAR292/32/2/3
Date: 28 Dec 1699
Ann Elphick, singlewoman, and her child; to
Kingsnorth in Kent where she lived as a menial
servant with James Ottoway

Again, the majority of these documents are from Sussex.
Of the 34 catalogue entries for the name Elvidge, only
one was for a document dated pre-1700 and that was for
1589 in Kent. This would appear to be an isolated
incidence of this name in the south of England as all
other examples noted during this research have found
Elvidge in the north of the country.

In 1890 H B Guppy published his *Homes of Family
Names in Great Britain*, still the only published work on
surname distribution in Britain as a whole. His work
was based on printed genealogies and a survey of
county directories for the 1880s, in which he looked
especially at the names of farmers, reasoning that they
were among the most stable groups in society.

Guppy restricted his study to names which
appeared in a proportion of 7:10,000 or higher. He found
the name Elvidge in Lincolnshire in a proportion of
8:10,000. Guppy suggested that the name was restricted

mainly to Lincoln itself and that the name was peculiar, and mostly confined, to the county.

We consulted George F Black's *The Surnames of Scotland* (1966), Edward MacLysaght's *Guide to Irish Surnames* (1965) and *The Surnames of Ireland* (1973), Sir Robert E Matheson's *Special Report on the Surnames of Ireland* (1968), T J Morgan and Prys Morgan's *Welsh Surnames* (1985) and J J Kneen's *The Personal Names of the Isle of Man* (1937) but found no mention of the name Elphick in any of these works. This suggests its confinement to England.

Elsdon C Smith's *American Surnames* (1986) makes no mention of Elphick or any of its variants. Our research in census indexes found several incidences of the surname in American records, but not in great numbers.

A survey of a cross section of parish registers for the years 1601 and 1602 was carried out in 1910 by F K and S Hitching; incidences of a particular surname are noted by parish and county, although with no indication of numbers of references. We found no reference at all to the name Elphick etc.

Scottish records of births, baptisms, marriages and deaths are indexed online for the period 1553 to 1953. Using this index we found very few entries for the name:

Old Parish Register Index of Births & Christenings 1553-1854

Elphick   1
Elvidge   1

Statutory Registration Index to Births 1855-1903
Elphick   6

Statutory Registration Index to Marriages 1855-1929
Elphick   7
Elvidge   3

Statutory Registration Index to Deaths 1855-1954
Elphick   14
Elvidge   6

These few entries may be strays as our searches in other Scottish sources had found similarly low numbers.

A useful guide to the distribution of surnames for the sixteenth, seventeenth and eighteenth centuries in England is provided by the indexes to wills proved, and administrations granted, at the Prerogative Court of (the Archbishop of) Canterbury, in London, which had superior jurisdiction over local ecclesiastical courts where wills were proved until 1858. The PCC thus provides a national index, although it is not a completely representative one, as testators whose wills were proved in the PCC were mostly among the wealthier members of society, and a disproportionate number of them were from London or Middlesex. A search of the online index found the following entries:

1560   John Elfeck of Seaford, Sussex
1579   Margaret Elpffik or Elphick of Yalding, Kent
1580   Robert Elphicke of Blatchington, Sussex
1602   Edmunde Elphick yeoman of Alciston, Sussex
1613   Thomas Elphicke yeoman of Ringmer, Sussex

1640	Richard Elphicke yeoman of Chiddingly, Sussex
1645	John Elphick gentleman of Petworth, Sussex
1646	Edward Elphicke
1648	Anne Elphicke widow of Southease, Sussex
1652	Mary Elphick spinster of Seaford, Sussex
1658	John Elphick yeoman of Hellingley, Sussex
1659	Thomas Elphicke gentleman of Sutton, Sussex
1661	Elizabeth Elphicke widow of Seaford, Sussex
1662	George Elphicke or Elphick gentleman of Exceate, Sussex
1663	George Elphicke grocer, factor for the Right Honourable the Company of East India Merchants being now bound forth on a voyage upon their Account to the East Indies
1668	George Elphicke of Gray's Inn, Middlesex
1674	James Elphick of Saint Saviour Southwark, Surrey
1690	John Elphicke gentleman of Cliffords Inn, London
1702	Thomas Elphick gentleman of Hayes, Middlesex
1707	John Elphick ship carpenter of Stratford le Bow, Middlesex
1740	Frances Elphick widow of Ringmer, Sussex
1743	George Elphick gentleman of Alfriston, Sussex
1749	Edward Elphick tailor of Canterbury, Kent
1755	Peake Elphick, gentleman of Lewes, Sussex
1770	Richard Elvidge of the Good Ship London outward bound to the East Indies
1772	John Elvidge stone taylor of St Swithin, City of London
1785	Robert Elfick victualler of Beckley, Sussex
1796	John Elphick butcher of Crawley, Sussex
1797	William Elvidge mariner now belonging to His Majesty's Frigate Leda
1814	William Elfick seaman of His Majesty's Sloop Rose

1822	George Elphick breeches maker of St James Street, Middlesex
1826	Edward Elfick Olleson gentleman of Deal, Kent
1826	William Elphick breeches maker of St George Hanover Square, Middlesex
1829	James Elphick keeper of His Majesty's Park called Bushy Park of Hampton, Middlesex
1831	Walter Elphicke of Tenterden, Kent
1836	Charles Elphick conveyancer of Horsham, Sussex
1837	William Elphick butcher of Cobham, Surrey
1838	Thomas Elvidge licensed victualler of Castle Mark Lane, City of London
1842	Emma Elphick of Stratford, Sussex
1842	William Elvidge gentleman of Lewisham, Kent
1849	William Elphick butcher of Brixton, Surrey
1850	Eliza Elphicke spinster of Tenterden, Kent
1850	Jane or Mary Elphick widow of Camberwell, Surrey
1852	Sarah Elphick widow of Horsham, Sussex
1854	Martha Elphick widow of Horsmonden, Kent
1855	Mary Elphick spinster of Walton upon Thames, Surrey

The majority of entries found were for testators from Sussex, with Kent and Surrey being the next most common counties, then Middlesex. Very few entries were found for the name Elvidge; those that were found were either Londoners or mariners and were from the latter end of the eighteenth century. Then at the beginning of the nineteenth century we find one Elvidge in Kent and another in London. We also found two Elphick entries in the indexes to Scottish wills and testaments between 1513 and 1901. (In Scotland, the practice of making a will differs slightly from England. As in England, the person making the will set down their instructions as to the disposal of their possessions and named their executor(s). The executor(s) were then confirmed by the court who drew up a document called a testament: the testament testamentar (for when the deceased died leaving a will) and testament dative (for when the deceased died intestate). This again reflects the low numbers found for this surname outside England.

For the nineteenth century, H B Guppy's survey has been mentioned above. Another important Victorian source is the *Return of Owners of Land* of 1873, sometimes known as the Modern Domesday Book. This source lists, county by county, every owner of an acre of land or more, with their residence (not necessarily the address of their property) and the acreage of their holding.

Return of Owners of Land 1873

County		Name
Essex	1	Elphic
	1	Elphicke
Kent	1	Elphiche
	1	Elphick
Lincolnshire	7	Elvidge
Nottinghamshire	2	Elvidge
Sussex	1	Elphick
Yorkshire, East	3	Elvidge
Yorkshire, West	2	Elvidge

Elvidge was found in Lincolnshire, Nottinghamshire and Yorkshire, all counties in the north of England. Entries for the name Elphick, also found as Elphic and Elphicke, were confined to the south-east where we also found a stray entry for Elphiche.

Decennial census returns were instituted in England, Scotland and Wales in 1801. Personal returns survive from 1841 onwards, with precise ages and birthplaces given from 1851 onwards. In the United States, decennial census records were instituted in 1790, but prior to 1850 only the head of the household was named, the other members being listed in age categories by gender; neither relationships nor birthplaces were stated. From 1850 onwards, each member of the household was named, but the information given varied from census to census. From 1880 onwards, the birthplace of each person's parents was given, thus supplying valuable genealogical information. Unfortunately, the 1890 census returns were destroyed by fire. All surviving census records are fully indexed.

1800
United States – Elvidge: 1

1810
United States – Affick: 1

1830
United States – Elvidge: 1

1840
United States – Elphick: 1

The US census records prior to 1850 only show the head of household and so the one entry found for the surname and its variants in 1800, 1810, 1830 and 1840, no doubt refers to numbers of persons rather than just one person in each year. The census taken in 1850 was the first US census to record all persons found in the household on census night and this fact is reflected in the figures noted for Elphick *etc* when we consulted the index to this particular record:

1850
United States
   Affick: 6
   Elfick: 1
   Elphick: 33

1851
England
   Alphege: 1
   Elfick: 37
   Elphic: 6
   Elphick: 669
   Elphicke: 1
   Elvidge: 386

As we can see, Elphick is by far the most common of the three variants of the name found in both England and America, with Affick coming second followed by Elfick with only one entry in America and Elvidge being the second most common variant in England.

1860
United States
   Elfick: 2
   Elphick: 26
   Elvidge: 29

1861
England
   Affick: 4
   Elfeck: 1
   Elfick: 37
   Elphick: 704
   Elphicke: 6
   Elvidge: 435

Scotland
Affick: 6
Elphick: 6

If we compare the 1860 US census to the English census taken the following year, we can see that there were relatively few (26) examples of the surname Elphick etc in America compared to England, where 704 Elphicks were recorded. Elvidge is the next most common name in this list with 435: only 29 persons used this name in America in 1860.

1870
United States
Affick: 8
Elfick: 7
Elphic: 25
Elphick: 49
Elphicke: 7
Elvidge: 30

1871
Channel Islands
Elphick: 3
England
Affick: 6
Elfick: 33
Elphic: 6
Elphick: 834
Elphicke: 10
Elvidge: 595
Scotland
Elphick: 7

In 1871, we find the name Elphick in the Channel Islands. The seven Elphicks found in Scotland in 1871 tally with the numbers found for this name in the marriage indexes of that country. Again, the most appearances found in England were for Elphick followed by Elvidge. As we can see from the American census records, taken the year before, the name was still rare in that country with only 49 entries noted for Elphick.

1880
United States
 Elfick: 19
 Elphic: 27
 Elphick: 54
 Elphicke: 8
 Elvidge: 75

1881
England
 Affick: 2
 Alphege: 1
 Elfick: 62
 Elphick: 993
 Elphicke: 7
 Elthicke: 3
 Elvidge: 578
Scotland
 Affick: 1
 Elphick: 7

The 1880 census index of America and the 1881 census index of England and Scotland, show a small increase across the board with the name Affick appearing in Scotland and Alphege in England.

1891
England
 Elfeck: 1
 Elfick: 39

Elphic: 7
Elphick: 1150
Elphicke: 12
Elvidge: 694
Scotland
Affick: 2
Elphick: 3

The 1890 census of America has been lost but the census index for England again shows a steady increase in the numbers recorded for the names Elphick and Elvidge but with a drop in the numbers of Elficks found.

1900
United States
Affick: 2
Elphic: 27
Elphick: 94
Elphicke: 4
Elvidge: 134

1901
England
Affick: 1
Elfeck: 1
Elfick: 52
Elphic: 5
Elphick: 1353
Elphicke: 14
Elvidge: 732
Scotland
Elphick: 4
Wales
Elphick: 6

In 1901, we found our first example of the name Elphick in Wales, with six persons of that name found resident in the country on census night. The numbers of persons recorded for Elphick and Elvidge have again risen slightly and we are still seeing very few entries for the other, more rare, variants of this name in both England and America.

1910 (Heads of Household)
United States
Affick: 2
Elphic: 14
Elphick: 48
Elvidge: 57

1920 (Heads of Household)
United States
Affick: 1
Elphic: 1
Elphick: 69
Elphicke: 1
Elvidge: 66

1930
United States
Alphege: 1
Elfick: 1
Elphic: 19
Elphick: 174
Elphicke: 1
Elvidge: 247

America allows access to census records up to, and including, 1930. The 1910 and 1920 census indexes record only heads of household and so the numbers recorded for surnames in these two records are not indicative of the numbers of persons actually using the names in those years. By 1930, we can see a truer representation of the surname Elphick in America and, again, the numbers for all variants are low but surprisingly the surname Elvidge is now more common in that country than Elphick.

Printed Genealogies

A search of various bibliographies of printed genealogies and family histories found three entries:

Alphegh
T E Sharpe *A Royal Descent* (London, 1875) 4to, 123

Elfeck
Berry's *Sussex Genealogies* 320, 372

Elphick
Sussex Archaeological Collections (Sussex
   Archaeological Society) First Series, volume vii,
   page 131

Heraldry

One coat of arms has been granted to a man named Elphick:

> **Elphick** – Argent on a chevron between three eagles with two heads gules as many plates

Summary

To conclude, the name Elphick has evolved from an Old English personal name which was recorded in a number of forms, *Ælfech* being one example: this name derives from *Ælf* and *hēah* meaning 'elf' and 'high'. A number of variants for the surname have been found during our research, the most prevalent being Elvidge, which appears to be more common in the north of England. Elphick, the dominant form of the name in England, is found mainly in the south-east of England, primarily in Kent and Sussex, although it has spread throughout England. It is very rare in Scotland, Wales and the Channel Islands. In the 1930s, Elvidge was the dominant form in America, but the name in all its forms remains rare in that country.

Sources Consulted

P H Reaney, *The Origins of English Surnames* (London: Routledge & Kegan Paul, 1967)

P H Reaney & R M Wilson, *A Dictionary of British Surnames* (Oxford: Oxford University Press, 3rd edition, 1995)

P H Reaney, *Dictionary of British Surnames* (London: Routledge & Kegan Paul, 2nd edition, 1976)

P Hanks & F Hodges, *A Dictionary of Surnames* (Oxford University Press, 1988)

M A Lower, *Patronymica Brittanica* (London, 1860)

C W Bardsley, *Dictionary of English and Welsh Surnames* (1901: reprinted, Baltimore: Genealogical Publishing Co, 1967)

C L'Estrange Ewen, *Guide to the Origin of British Surnames* (London: John Gifford, 1938)

H B Guppy, Homes of Family Names in Great Britain (London, 1890)

Ernest Weekley, *The Romance of Names* (London: John Murray, 2nd edition, 1917)

Ernest Weekley, *Surnames* (London: John Murray, 1917)

George F Black, *The Surnames of Scotland* (New York Public Library, 1946)

Edward McLysaght, *The Surnames of Ireland* (Dublin: Irish University Press, 1977)

T J & Prys Morgan, *Welsh Surnames* (Cardiff: University of Wales Press, 1985)

F K & S Hitching, *References to English Surnames in 1601* (Walton on Thames: Bernau, 1910)

F K & S Hitching, *References to English Surnames in 1602* (Walton on Thames: Bernau, 1911)

Debrett's People of Today (Debrett's Peerage Limited: London, 1996)

The Oxford Dictionary of National Biography (online, 2004–2014)

The Concise Dictionary of National Biography, Part II, 1901–1950, (Oxford, 1961)

Burke's Family Index (London: Burke's Peerage Limited, 1976)

H R Moulton, *Palaeography, Genealogy & Topography* (Sale Catalogue, 1930)

Index to Prerogative Court of Canterbury Wills (The National Archives: online)

G W Marshall, *The Genealogist's Guide* (1903; reprinted, Baltimore: GPC 1973)

J B Whitmore, *A Genealogical Guide* (London, 1953)

Charles Bridge, *An Index to Pedigrees* (London, 1867)

Geoffrey B Barrow, *The Genealogist's Guide* (London: Research Publishing Co, 1977)

Sir Bernard Burke, *The General Armory* (London, 1884)

C R Humphrey-Smith, editor, *Burke's General Armory Volume II*, (Tabard Press, 1973)

The Return of Owners of Land (1873)

Eilert Ekwall, *The Concise Oxford Dictionary of English Place-Names* (Oxford: Clarendon Press, 4th edition, 1960)

E G Withycombe, *The Oxford Dictionary of English Christian Names* (Oxford: Clarendon Press, 2nd edition, 1950)

W J Hardy & W Page, *A Calendar to the Feet of Fines for London and Middlesex: Vol 1 Richard I – Richard III (1189–1485)* (London, 1892)

Richard McKinley, *The Surnames of Oxfordshire* (English Surnames Series III: Leopard's Head Press, 1977)

Richard McKinley, *The Surnames of Sussex* (English Surnames Series V: Leopard's Head Press, 1988)

Richard McKinley, *The Surnames of Lancashire* (English Surnames Series IV: Leopard's Head Press, 1981)

Richard McKinley, *Norfolk and Suffolk Surnames in the Middle Ages* (English Surnames Series II: Phillimore, 1975)

R A McKinley, *A History of British Surnames* (Longman, 1990)

George Redmonds, *Yorkshire West Riding* (English Surnames Series I: Phillimore, 1973)

Mr Avenell, *The Norman People* (London, 1874)

Debrett's Heraldry (London, 1933)

J P Brooke-Little, revised, *Boutell's Heraldry* (Frederick Warne: London, 1970)

Indexes to 1841–1891 Census Returns of England and Wales (The National Archives/*Ancestry.com*)

ScotlandsPeople: Indexes to Old Parish Registers, Testaments, Statutory Registers

Access to Archives (The National Archives: online)